The Baking Book

Classic Cookies, Novel Treats, Brownies, Bars, and More

Beverly M. Morones

PIES AND PASTRY

PUFF PASTE OR BLAETTER TEIG

To make good puff paste one must have all the ingredients cold. Use a marble slab if possible and avoid making the paste on a warm, damp day. It should be made in a cool place as it is necessary to keep the paste cold during the whole time of preparation. This recipe makes two pies or four crusts, and requires one-half pound of butter and one-half teaspoon of salt, one-half pound of flour and one-fourth to one-half cup of ice-water.

Cut off one-third of the butter and put the remaining two-thirds in a bowl of ice-water. Divide this into four equal parts; pat each into a thin sheet and set them away on ice. Mix and sift flour and salt; rub the reserved butter into it and make as stiff as possible with ice-water. Dust the slab with flour; turn the paste upon it; knead for one minute, then stand it on ice for five minutes. Roll the cold paste into a square sheet about one-third of an inch thick; place the cold batter in the centre and fold the paste over it, first from the sides and then the ends, keeping the shape square and folding so that the butter is completely covered and cannot escape through any cracks as it is rolled. Roll out to one-fourth inch thickness, keeping the square shape and folding as before, but without butter. Continue rolling and folding, enclosing a sheet of butter at every alternate folding until all four sheets are used. Then turn the folded side down and roll in one direction into a long narrow strip, keeping the edges as straight as possible. Fold the paste over, making three even layers. Then roll again and fold as before. Repeat the process until the dough has had six turns. Cut into the desired shapes and place on the ice for twenty minutes or longer before putting in the oven.

If during the making the paste sticks to the board or pin, remove it immediately and stand it on the ice until thoroughly chilled. Scrape the board clean; rub with a dry cloth and dust with fresh flour before trying again. Use as little flour as possible in rolling, but use enough to keep the paste dry. Roll with a light, even, long stroke in every direction, but never work the rolling-pin back and forth as that movement toughens the paste and breaks the bubbles of air.

The baking of puff paste is almost as important as the rolling, and the oven must be very hot, with the greatest heat at the bottom, so that the paste will rise before it browns. If the paste should begin to scorch, open the drafts at once and cool the temperature by placing a pan of ice-water in the oven.

FLEISCHIG PIE CRUST

For shortening; use drippings and mix with goose, duck or chicken fat. In the fall and winter, when poultry is plentiful and fat, save all drippings of poultry fat for pie-crust. If you have neither, use rendered beef fat.

Take one-half cup of shortening, one and one-half cups of flour. Sifted pastry flour is best. If you have none at hand take two tablespoons of flour off each cup after sifting; add a pinch of salt. With two knives cut the fat into the sifted flour until the shortening is in pieces as small as peas. Then pour in six or eight tablespoons of cold water; in summer use ice-water; work with the knife until well mixed (never use the hand). Flour a board or marble slab, roll the dough out thin, sprinkle with a little flour and put dabs of soft drippings here and there, fold the dough over and roll out thin again and spread with fat and sprinkle with flour, repeat this and then roll out not too thin and line a pie-plate with this dough. Always cut dough for lower crust a little larger than the upper dough and do not stretch the dough when lining pie-pan or plate.

If fruit is to be used for the filling, brush over top of the dough with white of egg slightly beaten, or sprinkle with one tablespoon of bread crumbs to prevent the dough from becoming soggy.

Put in the filling, brush over the edge of pastry with cold water, lay the second round of paste loosely over the filling; press the edges together lightly, and trim, if needed. Cut several slits in the top crust or prick it with a fork before putting it in place.

Bake from thirty-five to forty-five minutes until crust is a nice brown.

A gas stove is more satisfactory for baking pies than a coal stove as pies require the greatest heat at the bottom.

The recipe given above makes two crusts. Bake pies having a cooked filling in a quick oven and those with an uncooked filling in a moderate oven. Let pies cool upon plates on which they were made because slipping them onto cold plates develops moisture which always destroys the crispness of the lower crust.

TO MAKE AND BAKE A MERINGUE

To beat and bake a meringue have cold, fresh eggs, beat the whites until frothy; add to each white one level tablespoon of powdered sugar. Beat until so stiff that it can be cut with a knife. Spread on the pie and bake with, the oven door open until a rich golden brown. Too much sugar causes a meringue to liquefy; if not baked long enough the same effect is produced.

PIE CRUST (MERBERTEIG)

Rub one cup of butter to a cream, add four cups of sifted flour, a pinch of salt and a tablespoon of brown sugar; work these together until the flour looks like sand, then take the yolk of an egg, a wine-glass of brandy, one-half cup of ice-water and work it into the flour lightly. Do not use the hands; knead with a knife or wooden spoon, knead as little as possible. If the dough is of the right consistency no flour will be required when rolling out the dough. If it is necessary to use flour use as little as possible. Work quickly, handle dough as little as possible and bake in a hot oven. Follow directions given with Fleischig Pie Crust. Fat may be substituted for butter in the above recipe.

PARVE, COOKIE AND PIE DOUGH

Sift into a mixing-bowl one and one-half cups of flour and one-half teaspoon of baking-powder. Make a depression in the centre; into this pour a generous half cup of oil and an exact half cup of very cold (or ice) water; add pinch of salt, mix quickly with a fork, divide in two portions; do not knead, but roll on a well-floured board, spread on pans, fill and bake at once in a quick oven.

No failure is possible if the formula is accurately followed and these things observed; ingredients cold, no kneading or re-rolling; dough must not stand, but the whole process must be completed as rapidly as possible.

Do not pinch or crimp the edge of this or any other pie. To do so makes a hard edge that no one cares to eat. Instead, trim the edges in the usual way, then place the palms of the hand on opposite sides of the pie and raise the dough until the edges stand straight up. This prevents all leakage and the crust is tender to the last morsel.

TARTLETS

Roll puff paste one-eighth of an inch thick; cut it into squares; turn the points together into the middle and press slightly to make them stay. Bake until thoroughly done; place a spoonful of jam in the centre of each; cover the jam with meringue and brown the meringue in a quick oven.

By brushing the top of the paste with beaten egg, diluted with one teaspoon of water, a glazed appearance may be obtained.

BANBURY TARTS

Cut one cup of seeded muscatel raisins and one cup of nuts in small pieces, add one cup of sugar, one well-beaten egg, one tablespoon of water, the juice and grated rind of one lemon. Mix well. Line patty-pans with pie dough, fill with mixture and bake until crust is brown.

FRUIT TARTLETS

If canned fruit is used, take a large can of any kind of fruit, drain all the syrup off and put in a saucepan with an equal quantity of sugar. Cook until it forms a syrup, then pour in the fruit, which has been stoned (if necessary), and cook until the whole is a syrupy mass.

Line a pie-plate with rich paste, sprinkle cornstarch lightly over the bottom crust and fill with cherries and regulate the quantity of sugar you scatter over them by their sweetness. Bake with an upper crust, secure the edges well by pinching firmly together. Eat cold.

CHERRY PIE, No. 2

Pick the stems out of your cherries and put them in an earthen crock, then set them in the oven until they get hot. Take them out and seed them. Make tarts with or without tops and sugar to your taste. The heating of the fruit gives the flavor of the seed, which is very rich, but the seeding of them while hot is not a delightful job. Made this way they need no water for juice.

SNOWBALLS

Pare and core nice large baking apples, fill the holes with some preserves or jam, roil the apples in sugar and cover with a rich pie crust and bake. When done, cover with a boiled icing and set back in the oven, leaving both doors open to let the icing dry.

BLACKBERRY AND CURRANT PIE

When ready to make the pie, mix as much fruit in a bowl as required, sweeten, stirring the sugar through the berries and currants lightly with a spoon. Dust in a little flour and stir it through the fruit. Cut one of the pieces of pastry in halves, dust the pastry-board with flour and roll the lump of pastry out very thin, cover the pie-plate, a big deep one, with the pastry, trim off the edges with a knife, cutting from you. Fill the dish with the fruit, dust the surface well with flour. Roll out the other piece for the top crust, fold it over the rolling pin, cut a few gashes in it for a steam vent.

Carefully put on the top crust, trim it well about the edge of the pie-plate. Press it closely together with the end of your thumb or with a pastry knife and stand the pie in a moderate oven and bake till the surface is a delicate brown. Then remove the pie and let it stand until it is cool.

The top crust may be made lattice fashion by cutting the pastry in strips, but it will not be as good as between two closed crusts.

CUSTARD PIE

Line the pie-plate with a rich crust. Beat up four eggs light with one-half cup of sugar, a pinch of salt, one pint of milk and grated nutmeg or grated lemon peel, and pour in shell and bake in slow oven.

CREAM PIE

First line a pie-plate with puff paste and bake, and then make a cream of the yolks of four eggs, a little more than a pint of milk, one tablespoon of cornstarch and four tablespoons of sugar, and flavor with two teaspoons of vanilla. Pour on crust and bake; beat up the whites with two tablespoons of powdered sugar and half a teaspoon of cream of tartar. Spread on top of pie and set back in the oven until baked a light brown.

COCOANUT PIE

Line a pie-plate with puff paste and fill with the following custard: Butter size of an egg, creamed with one cup of granulated sugar, one tablespoon of flour, three-fourths cup of grated cocoanut, one tablespoon of milk, vanilla, pinch of salt, and the beaten whites of three eggs.

COCOANUT LEMON PIE

Beat the yolks of six eggs and one cup of sugar until very light, squeeze in the juice of three lemons and the rind of two of them, stir well, then add one-half of a cocoanut grated, and lastly add the whites of six eggs, beaten to a stiff froth. Line a deep pie-plate with rich pastry, sprinkle a little flour over it, pour in the lemon mixture and bake. This makes one pie in deep pie-plate.

LEMON PIE, No. 1

Cover the reverse side of a deep pie-plate with a rich puff paste, and bake a light brown. Remove from the oven until the filling is prepared. Take a large juicy lemon, grate and peel and squeeze out every drop of juice. Now take the lemon and put it into a cup of boiling water to extract every particle of juice. Put the cup of water on to boil with the lemon juice and grated peel, and a cup of sugar; beat up the yolks of four eggs very light and add to this gradually the boiling lemon juice. Return to the kettle and boil. Then wet a teaspoon of cornstarch with a very little cold water, and add also a teaspoon of butter and when the boiling mixture has thickened remove from the fire and let it cool. Beat up the whites of the eggs to a very stiff froth, add half of the froth to the lemon mixture and reserve the other half for the top of the pie. Bake the lemon cream in the baked pie-crust. Add a few tablespoons of powdered sugar and half a teaspoon of cream of tartar to the remaining beaten whites. If you desire to have the meringue extra thick, add the whites of one or more eggs. When the pie is baked take from the oven just long enough to spread the meringue over the top, and set back for two or three minutes, leaving the oven doors open just the least bit, so as not to have it brown too quickly.

LEMON PIE, No. 2

Line a deep pie-plate with nice crust, then prepare a filling as follows: After removing the crust from two slices of bread about two inches thick, pour over it one cup of boiling water; add one dessertspoon of butler, and beat until the bread is well soaked and smooth; then add the juice and rind of one lemon, one cup of sugar, the yolks of two eggs, well beaten, and a little salt; mix well; fill pie with mixture and bake in hot oven until firm. Beat white of two eggs to a stiff froth, add four tablespoons of powdered sugar and spread on top and brown.

MOCK MINCE PIE

Pare, core, and chop fine eight tart apples. Add one cup of seedless raisins, one-half cup of currants, one ounce of chopped citron, one-half teaspoon each of cinnamon, cloves, spice and mace, a tiny bit of salt and grated nutmeg. Pour over whole one tablespoon of brandy, and juice and rind of one lemon. Line bottom and sides of plate with crust, fill in with mixture, and put strips of dough across.

MINCE PIE

Boil two pounds lean, fresh beef. When cold, chop fine. Add one-half pound chopped suet, shredded very fine, and all gristle removed. Mix in a bowl two pounds of seeded raisins, two pounds of currants, one-half pound of citron, chopped very fine. Two tablespoons of cinnamon, two tablespoons of mace, one grated nutmeg, one tablespoon of cloves, allspice, and salt. Mix this with meat and suet. Then take two cups of white wine, two and one-half pounds of brown sugar. Let stand. Chop fine four apples, and add meat to fruits. Then mix wine with whole, stir well, and put up in small stone jars. This will keep all winter in a cool place. Let stand at least two days before using. Line pie-plates with a rich crust, fill with mince meat mixture, put a rich paste crust on top, or strips if preferred, prick slightly and bake. Serve warm, not hot.

PUMPKIN PIE

Press through a sieve one pint of stewed pumpkin, add four eggs and a scant cup of sugar. Beat yolks and sugar together until very thick and add one pint of milk to the beaten eggs. Then add the pressed pumpkin, one-half teaspoon of cinnamon, less than one-half teaspoon of mace and grated nutmeg. Stir the stiffly-beaten whites in last. Bake in a very rich crust without cover.

GRAPE PIE

Squeeze out the pulps and put them in one vessel, the skins into another. Then simmer the pulp a little and press it through a colander to separate the seeds. Then put the skins and pulps together and they are ready for the pies.

HUCKLEBERRY PIE

Line a pie-plate with rich pastry. Pick, clean and wash one pint of huckleberries, drain and lay them thickly on the crust. Sprinkle thickly with sugar, lightly with cinnamon, and drop bits of butter over the top. Bake a nice even brown.

PEACH CREAM TARTS

One cup of butter, and a little salt; cut through just enough flour to thoroughly mix, a cup of ice-water, one whole egg and the yolks of two eggs mixed with a tablespoon of brown sugar. Add to the flour in which you have previously sifted two teaspoons of baking-powder. Handle the dough as little as possible in mixing. Bake in round rings in a hot oven until a light brown. When baked, sift pulverized sugar over the top and fill the hollow centre with a compote of peaches. Heap whipped cream or ice-cream on top of each one, the latter being preferable.

MOCK CHERRY PIE

Cover the bottom of pie-plate with rich crust; reserve enough for upper crust. For filling use two cups of cranberries, cut in halves; one cup of raisins, cut in pieces; two cups of sugar, butter the size of walnut. Dredge with flour, sprinkle with water. Bake thirty minutes in a moderate oven.

PEACH CREAM PIE

Line a pie-plate with a rich crust and bake, then fill with a layer of sweetened grated peaches which have had a few pounded peach kernels added to them. Whip one cup of rich cream, sweeten and flavor and spread over the peaches. Set in ice-chest until wanted.

PEACH PIE, No. 1

Line a pie-plate with a rich pie-crust, cover thickly with peaches that have been pared and sliced fine (canned peaches may be used when others are not to be had), adding; sugar and cover with strips of dough; bake quickly.

PEACH PIE, No. 2

Pare, stone, and slice the peaches. Line a deep pie-plate with a rich paste, sprinkle a little flour over the bottom crust and lay in your fruit, sprinkle sugar liberally over them in proportion to their sweetness. Add a few peach kernels, pounded fine, to each pie and bake with crossbars of paste across the top. If you want it extra fine, with the whites of three eggs to a stiff froth and sweeten with about four tablespoons of pulverized sugar, adding one-fourth of a teaspoon of cream tartar, spread over the pie and return to the oven until the meringue is set. Eat cold.

PINEAPPLE PIE, No. 1

Line your pie-plate with a rich paste, slice pineapples as thin as possible, sprinkle sugar over them abundantly and put flakes of sugar here and there. Cover and bake.

You may make pineapple pies according to any of the plain apple pie recipes.

PINEAPPLE PIE, No. 2

Pare and core the pineapple and cut into small slices and sprinkle abundantly with sugar and set it away in a covered dish to draw enough juice to stew the pineapple in. Bake two shells on perforated pie-plates of a rich pie dough. When the pineapple is stewed soft enough to mash, mash it and set it away to cool. When the crust is baked and cool whip half a pint of sweet cream and mix with the pineapple and fill in the baked shell.

PRUNE AND RAISIN PIE

Use one-half pound of prunes, cooked until soft enough to remove the stones. Mash with a fork and add the juice in which they have been cooked; one-half cup of raisins, cooked in a little water for a few minutes until soft; add to the prune mixture with one-half cup of sugar; a little ground clove or lemon juice improves the flavor. Bake with two crusts.

PRUNE PIE

Make a rich pie paste. After the paste is rolled out thin and the pie-plate lined with it, put in a layer of prunes that have been stewed the day before, with the addition of several slices of lemon and no sugar.

Split the prunes in halves and remove the pits before laying them on the pie crust.

After the first layer is in sprinkle it well with sugar, then pour over the sugar three or four tablespoons of the prune juice and dust the surface lightly with flour.

Repeat this process till there are three layers, then cut enough of the paste in strips to cover the top of the fruit with a lattice crust and bake the pie in a rather quick oven.

Few pies can excel this in daintiness of flavor.

PLUM PIE

Select large purple plums, about fifteen plums for a good-sized pie; cut them in halves, remove the kernels and dip each half in flour. Line your pie-tin with a rich paste and lay in the plums, close together, and sprinkle thickly with a whole cup of sugar. Lay strips of paste across the top, into bars, also a strip around the rim, and press all around the edge with a pointed knife or fork, which will make a fancy border. Sift powdered sugar on top. Damson pie is made in the same way. Eat cold.

RHUBARB PIE

Make a very rich crust, and over the bottom layer sprinkle a large tablespoon of sugar and a good teaspoon of flour. Fill half-full of rhubarb that has been cut up, scatter in one-fourth cup of strawberries or raspberries, sprinkle with more sugar and flour, and then proceed as before. Over the top dot bits of butter and another dusting of flour. Use a good cup of sugar to a pie. Pinch the crusts together well after wetting them, to prevent the juice, which should be so thick that it does not soak through the lower crust at all, from cooking out.

STRAWBERRY PIE

Make a rich fleischig pie-crust and bake on the reverse side of pie-pan. Pick a quart of berries, wash and drain, then sugar. Take the yolks of four eggs beaten well with one-half cup of sugar and stir the beaten whites gently into this mixture. Pour over strawberries. Put in pie-crust and bake until brown. This mixture with most all fruit pies will be found delicious.

SWEET POTATO PIE

Measure one cup of mashed, boiled sweet potatoes. Thin with one pint of sweet milk. Beat three whole eggs very light with one-half cup of sugar. Mix with sweet potatoes. Season with one-quarter of a nutmeg grated, one teaspoon of cinnamon, and one-half teaspoon of lemon extract. Line pie-plate with crust, fill with mixture, and bake in quick oven.

VINEGAR PIE

Line a pie-plate with a rich crust and fill with the following mixture: One cup of vinegar, two of water and two cups of sugar, boil; add a lump of butter and enough cornstarch to thicken; flavor with lemon essence and put in a shell and bake.

MOHNTORTE

Line a form with a rich puff paste, fill with half a pound of white mohn (poppy seed) which has been previously soaked in milk and then ground. Add a quarter of a pound of sugar and the yolks of six eggs; stir all together in one direction until quite thick. Then stir the beaten whites, to which add two ounces of sifted flour and a quarter of a pound of melted butter. Fill and bake. When done, frost either with vanilla or rose frosting.

RAISIN PIE

Line pie pan with rounds of rich pastry, fill with same mixture as for "Banbury Tarts"; cover with a round of pastry and bake a light brown.

RAISIN AND RHUBARB PIE

COOKIES

In baking small cakes and cookies, grease the pans. If the pans cool before you can take off the cookies, set back on stove for a few moments. The cakes will then slip off easily. Sponge, drop cakes, anise cakes, etc., are better baked on floured pans.

A whole raisin, an almond blanched, a piece of citron or half a walnut may be used to decorate.

A good way to glaze is, when cookies are about baked, rub over with a brush dipped in sugar and water and return to oven a moment.

FILLED BUTTER CAKES (DUTCH STUFFED MONKEYS)

Make a paste by working three-fourths pound of butter into one pound of flour, with three-fourths pound of light brown sugar, one egg, one teaspoon of cinnamon, and a pinch of salt.

Next mix one-half pound of finely chopped citron peel with one-half pound of ground almonds, and three ounces of butter. Then flavor with one-half teaspoon of vanilla and bind with the yolks of two eggs.

Roll out the dough and divide into two parts. Place one-half on a well-buttered flat pan and spread the mixture over it and cover with the other half of the paste. Brush with beaten egg, sprinkle with poppy seed and bake in a moderately quick oven for one-half hour. When done let cool and then cut into square or oblong pieces.

The butter cakes may be made of one layer of dough sprinkled with citron and almonds and some poppy seed.

SUGAR COOKIES

In a mixing bowl put a cup of sweet butter and two cups of granulated sugar; beat these ingredients to a cream, then add three eggs, grated lemon rind, and four tablespoons of brandy. Beat the added ingredients thoroughly with the others till the mixture is smooth and creamy. Sift three cups of flour in a big bowl with a teaspoon of salt and three teaspoons of baking-powder; stir this a little at a time in the bowl with the other ingredients, until the mixture is a light dough, just stiff enough to roll out. If there is not enough flour, sift more in to make the dough the desired stiffness; then dust the pastry board well with flour, put part of the dough on the board, toss it lightly with your hands from side to side till the dough is covered with flour. Then dust the rolling-pin well with flour and roll the dough very thin; cut it in shapes with a cookie cutter, lift each cookie up carefully with a pancake turner, slip them quickly in a big baking-pan, the inside of which has been well rubbed with flour, and bake them in a moderate oven till light brown.

Just a moment before taking the pan out of the oven sprinkle the surface of the cookies lightly with granulated sugar. When a little cool take the cookies out of the pan with the pancake turner and lay them on a big platter. When they are cold put the cookies in a stone crock.

It is a good plan to have two or three baking-pans so, while one panful is baking, another may be filled and be ready to put in the oven when the other is removed. Only put enough dough on the pastry board at a time to roll out nicely on it.

OLD-FASHIONED HAMBURGER COOKIES

Take one pound of butter one pound of sugar, yolks of six eggs, hard-boiled, and flour enough to make a dough that is not too stiff.

Dissolve three cents worth of ammonia (hartshorn) in scalded milk. Place the ammonia in a large bowl and pour one cup of scalding milk over it. After this has cooled add it to the dough with one-half cup of cold milk. Flavor to taste. Flour the pans and the cookie dough. Roll and proceed as with sugar cookies.

MOTHER'S DELICIOUS COOKIES (MERBER KUCHEN)

Take ten boiled eggs and two raw ones, one pound of best butter, half a pound of almonds, one lemon, some cinnamon one wineglass of brandy, one pound of pulverized sugar and about one pound and a half of flour. This quantity makes one hundred cookies, and like fruit cake, age improves them, in other words, the older the better. Now to begin with: Set a dish of boiling water on the stove, when it boils hard, break the eggs carefully, one at a time, dropping the whites in a deep porcelain dish, and set away in a cool place. Take each yolk as you break the egg and put it in a half shell, and lay it in the boiling water until you have ten boiling. When boiled hard take them up and lay them on a plate to cool. In the meantime, cream the butter with a pound of pulverized sugar, add the grated peel of a lemon, a teaspoon of cinnamon and half of the almonds, which have been blanched and pounded or grated (reserve the other half for the top of the cookies, which should not be grated, but pounded). Add the hard-boiled yolks, which must be grated, and the two raw eggs, sift in the flour, and add the brandy. Beat up the whites of the twelve eggs very stiff, add half to the dough, reserving the other half, but do not make the dough stiff, as it should be so rich that you can hardly handle it. Flour the baking-board well, roll out about an eighth of an inch thick. Now spread with the reserved whites of eggs, reserving half again, as you will have to roll out at least twice on a large baking-board. Sprinkle well with the pounded almonds after you have spread the beaten whites of the eggs on top, also sugar and cinnamon. Cut with a cookie-cutter. Have at least five large pans greased ready to receive them. See that you have a good fire. Time to bake, five to ten minutes. Pack them away when cold in a stone jar or tin cake-box. These cookies will keep a long time.

VANILLA COOKIES

Rub one cup of butter and one cup of sugar to a cream; add two eggs and two level teaspoons of baking-powder, flour enough to make a dough. Flavor with vanilla, roll very thin, spread with beaten white of egg and sugar. Proceed as for sugar cookies.

OLD-FASHIONED MOLASSES COOKIES

Put in a mixing bowl one generous cup of butter which has stood in a warm place until quite soft; add two cups of New Orleans molasses; whip these ingredients to a foam; then add two teaspoons of powdered ginger, one teaspoon of powdered cinnamon and grate in half a large nutmeg; stir these spices well through the mixture; then dissolve two teaspoons of baking-soda in half a cup of hot water; stir it through the mixture, and last, stir in enough sifted flour to make a light dough just stiff enough to roll out.

Dust the pastry board well with flour and rub the rolling-pin well with flour; then flour the hands well, take out some of the dough, put it on the pastry board, quickly roll it out to the thickness of a quarter of an inch; cut the dough out with a round cutter, with or without scallops, and put them in well-floured baking-pans and bake in a slow oven till a golden brown.

SOUR MILK COOKIES

Take one cup of butter, one cup of sugar, two or three eggs, and two-thirds of a cup of sour milk. Dissolve a teaspoon of soda in a little hot water; add part of it at a time to the milk until it foams as you stir it. Be careful not to get in too much. Mix up soft only using flour sufficient to roll out thin. A teaspoon of cardamom seed may be sprinkled into the dough.

HUNGARIAN ALMOND COOKIES

Scant one-quarter of a pound of almonds, blanched and grated; scant one-half pound of sweet butter; not quite three-quarters of a pound of flour; a little sugar and a pinch of salt, and two yolks. Mix this well, pound the dough well with the rolling-pin, then roll out not too thin. Bake.

NUTMEG CAKES (PFEFFERNUESSE)

Sift one pound of flour and one pound of pulverized sugar into a large bowl, four eggs, a piece of citron grated or chopped very fine, also the peel of a lemon, one whole nutmeg grated, one tablespoon of ground cinnamon, one-half teaspoon of ground cloves, and half a teaspoon of allspice. Mix all thoroughly in a deep bowl. Sift a heaping teaspoon of baking-powder in with the flour. Work into little balls as large as hickory nuts with buttered or floured hands. Bake on waxed or buttered tins, an inch apart.

ANISE SEED COOKIES (SPRINGELE)

Four eggs, not separated, but thoroughly beaten, then add one and one-half cups of granulated sugar, and beat for thirty minutes; add two heaping cups of flour and fourteen drops of anise seed oil; drop from a teaspoon on well-buttered pans, and bake in a moderate oven. It will improve them to let them stand from two to three hours in the pans before baking.

CARDAMOM COOKIES

Boil six eggs hard. When cold shell and grate the yolks (reserve the whites for salads or to garnish vegetables), add one-half pound of sugar, the grated peel of a lemon and one-half wineglass of brandy. Stir in one-half pound of butter which has been worked to a cream. Sift in as much flour as you think will allow you to roll out the dough; take as little as possible, a little over half a pound, and flour the board very thick. Put in about two cents worth of cardamom seed and a little rosewater. Cut out with a fancy cake-cutter and brush with beaten egg. Sprinkle pounded almonds and sugar on top.

PURIM CAKES

Take two cups of flour, one tablespoon of sugar, add four eggs and two tablespoons of oil; knead all these together, roll out not very thin, cut in squares, close two sides, prick with a fork so they will not blister; put on tins and bake well. Then take one pound of honey, boil, and put the squares in this and let boil a bit; then drop in one-quarter pound of poppy seeds and put back on fire. When nice and brown sprinkle with a little cold water, take off and put on another dish so they do not stick to each other.

PARVE COOKIES

To one pound of flour take one teaspoon of baking-powder, four eggs, one-quarter pound of poppy seeds, three tablespoons of oil, two pounds of sugar and a little salt; knead not too stiff and put on tins and bake in hot oven till a nice brown. (Do not let burn.)

TEIGLECH

Mix one pound of flour, one teaspoon of baking-powder, three tablespoons of oil, and four eggs; knead very well. Roll out in strips three inches long, place on tins and bake. Take a pound of chopped nuts, one-half pound of honey, and one-half pound of sugar; mix thoroughly with wooden spoon and boil with the cakes until brown. Take off the stove; wet with cold water, spread out on board. When cold, pat with the hands to make thin and sprinkle with dry ginger.

HONEY CORN CAKES

Boil one pound of pure honey. Take one pound of cornmeal mixed with a little ground allspice, cloves, and pepper, add the boiled honey, make a loose batter, add one wineglass of brandy; mix all, and cool. Wet the hands with cold water, take pieces of the dough and knead until the dough comes clear from the hand; afterwards knead with white flour so it is not too hard; add one pound of chopped nuts, sprinkle flour on tins, spread dough, not too thin; leave the stove door open till it raises; then close door, and when done take out. Spread with brandy and cut in thin slices.

CROQUANTE CAKES (SMALL CAKES)

Blanch and cut in halves three-fourths pound of shelled almonds, and slice one-half pound of citron; mix well together and roll in a little flour; add to them three-fourths pound of sugar, then six eggs well beaten, and last the rest of the flour (three-fourths pound). Butter shallow pans, and put in the mixture about two inches thick; after it is baked in a quick oven slice cake in strips three-fourths of an inch wide and turn each piece. Put back in oven and bake a little longer. When cold put away in tin box.

KINDEL

Two pounds of soup fat rendered a day or two before using, three pints of flour, one teaspoon of salt, two-thirds cup of granulated sugar, one teaspoon of baking-powder, two teaspoons of vanilla, flour. Knead well, add enough beer to be able to roll. Let it stand two hours.

Roll, cut in long strips three inches wide. Fill with the following: One and one-half cups of brown sugar, two tablespoons of honey, two pounds of walnuts chopped fine, one pound of stewed prunes chopped fine, two cups of sponge cake crumbs, juice of one lemon, spices to taste, few raisins and currants, and a little citron chopped fine; add a little wine, a little chicken schmalz; heat a few minutes. You may use up remnants of jellies, jams, marmalades, etc. Put plenty of filling in centre of strips, fold over, with a round stick (use a wooden spoon), press the dough firmly three inches apart, then with a knife cut them apart. They will be the shape of the fig bars you buy. Grease the pan and the top of cakes, and bake in moderate oven. They will keep—the longer the better.

ALMOND MACAROONS, No. 1

Blanch half a pound of almonds, pound in mortar to a smooth paste, add one pound of pulverized sugar and the beaten whites of four eggs, and work the paste well together with the back of a spoon. Dip your hands in water and roll the mixture into balls the size of a hickory nut and lay on buttered or waxed paper an inch apart. When done, dip your hands in water and pass gently over the macaroons, making the surface smooth and shiny. Set in a cool oven three-quarters of an hour.

ALMOND MACAROONS, No. 2

Prepare the almonds by blanching them in boiling water. Strip them of the skins and lay them on a clean towel to dry. Grate or pound one-half pound of almonds, beat the whites of five eggs to a stiff, very stiff froth; stir in gradually three-quarters of a pound of pulverized sugar (use confectioner's sugar if you can get it), and then add the pounded almonds, to which add a tablespoon of rosewater or a teaspoon of essence of bitter almonds. Line a broad baking-pan with buttered or waxed paper and drop upon this half a teaspoon of the mixture at a time, allowing room enough to prevent their running together. Sift powdered sugar over them and bake in a quick oven to a delicate brown. If the mixture has been well beaten they will not run. Try one on a piece of paper before you venture to bake them all. If it runs add a little more sugar.

ALMOND MACAROONS WITH FIGS

Beat stiff the whites of three eggs, add one-half pound of sugar, and one-half pound of finely cut figs, one-half pound of either blanched almonds cut into long slices, or cut up walnuts. Heat a large pan, pass ironing-wax over surface, lay in waxed paper, and drop spoonfuls of mixture on paper, same distance apart. Bake very slowly in very moderate oven. Remove and let cool; then take paper out with the macaroons, turn over and place hot cloths on wrong; side, when cakes will drop off.

ALMOND STICKS—FLEISCHIG

Take one-half glass of fat, two eggs, four cups of flour, two teaspoons of baking-powder, one cup of water, one-half cup of sugar; knead lightly, and roll out not too thin. Two cups of sugar, mix with two teaspoons of cinnamon; one-half pound of grated almonds, one-half pound of small raisins (washed). Reserve one-half of the sugar and cinnamon, the nuts and raisins; brush the dough with melted fat and sprinkle with almonds and sugar. Put a little of the almond and raisin mixture around the edge and roll around twice. Cut in small pieces, brush every piece with fat, and roll in the sugar and almonds which has been reserved for this purpose. Place in greased pan and bake in hot oven.

ALMOND STICKS

Grind two cups of almonds and reserve one-quarter cup each of sugar and nuts, and an egg yolk for decorating. Cream one cup of butter, add three-fourths cup of sugar, then two whole eggs, almonds and two cups of flour. Roll thin and cut in strips or squares, with fluted cookie cutter. Brush with yolk, sprinkle with nuts and sugar, set aside, and bake in medium oven.

PLAIN WAFERS

Sift one cup of flour and one teaspoon of salt together. Chop in one tablespoon of butter, and add milk to make a very stiff dough; chop thoroughly and knead until smooth; make into small balls and roll each one into a thin wafer. Place in shallow greased and floured pans and bake in a hot oven until they puff and are brown.

POPPY SEED COOKIES (MOHN PLAETZCHEN)

Take an equal quantity of flour, sugar and butter, and mix it well by rubbing with the hollow of the hands until small grains are formed. Then add one cup of poppy seed, two eggs, and enough Rhine wine to hold the dough together. Roll out the dough on a well-floured board, about half a finger in thickness, cut into any shape desired.

CARAWAY SEED COOKIES

Beat three-quarters of a pound of butter and a pound of sugar to a cream; add three eggs, one saltspoon of salt, a gill of caraway seeds and a teaspoon of powdered mace, stirring all well together to a cream; then pour in a cup of sour milk in which a level teaspoon of baking-soda is stirred.

Hold the cup over the mixing bowl while stirring in the soda, as it will foam over the cup. Last of all stir in enough sifted flour to make a light dough, stiff enough to roll thin. Roll on a pastry board well dusted with flour. Cut in round shapes and place in baking-tins well rubbed with flour.

Sprinkle a little sugar over the cookies and bake them in a moderate oven till a light brown. When cool, carefully lift the cookies from the pans with a pancake turner.

CITRON COOKIES

Take one-half cup of butter and one cup and a half of sugar, and rub to a cream. Add two eggs, three-quarters of a cup of milk; one-half cup of citron, cut up very fine, one teaspoon of allspice and one of cloves. Sift one heaping teaspoon of baking-powder into enough flour to thicken. Make stiffer than ordinary cup cake dough; flavor to suit taste, and drop on large tins with a teaspoon. Grease the pans, and bake in a quick oven. The best plan is to try one on a plate. If the dough runs too much add more flour.

GINGER WAFERS

Take one cup of butter, one cup of sugar, one cup of molasses, half a cup of cold coffee, with two teaspoons of soda, one teaspoon of ginger, and flour enough to make a dough stiff enough to roll out thin. Shape with cutter and bake in quick oven.

ANISE ZWIEBACK

Take the yolks of five eggs, one-half pound of sugar, one tablespoon of water, vanilla, one-half pound of flour, one teaspoon of baking-powder, one-half of five cents worth anise seeds, and the beaten whites of the eggs. Butter square tins and bake. When cooled cut in strips one inch wide and toast on both sides.

HURRY UPS (OATMEAL)

Sift one cup of flour with two teaspoons of baking-powder, one teaspoon of salt, add one cup of rolled oats, one tablespoon of sugar and two tablespoons of melted butter, mix with one-half cup of milk.

Drop by teaspoons onto a greased pan, press well into each two or three raisins, or a split date and bake for twenty minutes in a hot oven. Can be served with butter, honey, or maple sugar.

PECAN, WALNUT, OR HICKORY NUT MACAROONS

Take one cup of pulverized sugar, and one cup of finely-pounded nut meats, the unbeaten whites of two eggs, two heaping teaspoons of flour, and one scant teaspoon of baking-powder. Mix these ingredients together and drop from a teaspoon which, you have previously dipped in cold water, upon buttered paper. Do not put them too near each other, for they always spread a great deal. Bake about fifteen minutes.

DATE MACAROONS

Stone thirty dates; chop them fine. Cut one-half pound of almonds lengthwise in slices, but do not blanch them. Beat the whites of two eggs until foamy, add one cup of powdered sugar, and beat until stiff; add the dates, then the almonds, and mix very thoroughly. Drop mixture with teaspoon in small piles on tins, one-half inch apart. Bake thirty minutes in a very slow oven or until dry. They are done when they leave the pan readily.

MANDELCHEN

Blanch two cups of almonds and dry them overnight. Grind very fine, add one-half cup of sugar and enough butter to knead into a very stiff paste. Roll very thin, cut in small rounds, place in baking-tin in moderate oven. When done, roll in grated almonds and powdered sugar.

COCOANUT KISSES

Beat the white of one egg; add one-half cup of sugar with a flavoring of vanilla, fold in one cup of shredded cocoanut, drop by teaspoonfuls on a well-greased baking-pan, inverted, and bake for about ten or twelve minutes in a slow oven. Remove from pan when cookies are cold.

CORNFLAKE COCOANUT KISSES

Mix the whites of two eggs, beaten stiff, with one-half cup of sugar, add one-half cup of shredded cocoanut, fold in two cups of corn flakes, a pinch of salt, one-half teaspoon of vanilla. Make and bake same as kisses above.

CHOCOLATE COOKIES

Beat whites of three eggs to a snow, add three-fourths cup of powdered sugar, one cup of ground sweet chocolate, one cup of walnuts chopped, three tablespoons of flour. Drop by teaspoonful on greased baking-tin. Bake in slow oven.

BASELER LOEKERLEIN (HONEY CAKES)

Take half a pound of strained honey, half a pound of sifted powdered sugar, half a pound of almonds (cut in half lengthwise), half a pound of finest flour, one ounce of citron (cut or chopped extremely fine), peel of a lemon, a little grated nutmeg, also a pinch of ground cloves and a wineglass of brandy. Set the honey and sugar over the fire together, put in the almonds, stir all up thoroughly. Next put in the spices and work into a dough. Put away in a cold place for a week, then roll about as thick as a finger. Bake in a quick oven and cut into strips with a sharp knife after they are baked (do this while hot), cut three inches long and two inches wide.

HONEY CAKES, No. 1

One pound of real honey, not jar; one cup of granulated sugar, four eggs, one tablespoon of allspice, three tablespoons of salad-oil, four cups of flour, well sifted; three teaspoons of baking-powder. Warm up or heat honey, not hot, just warm. Rub yolks well with sugar, beat whites to a froth, then mix ingredients, add flour and bake in moderate oven for one hour.

HONEY CAKES, No. 2

Three eggs, not separated, beaten with one cup of sugar, one cup of honey, one cup of blanched almonds chopped finely, one teaspoon each of allspice, cloves, and cinnamon, one cup of chocolate and flour enough to make a thick batter; one teaspoon of baking-soda. Spread very thin on square, buttered pans, bake in a hot oven, and when done, spread with a white icing, cut into squares, and put a half blanched almond in the centre of each square.

LEKACH

This recipe is one that is used in Palestine. It makes a honey cake not nearly as rich as those in the foregoing recipes for honey cakes, but will very nicely take the place of a sweet cracker to serve with tea.

Take three cups of sifted flour, one-quarter teaspoon of salt, add three eggs, one teaspoon of allspice, one teaspoon of soda, the grated rind and juice of one-half lemon and three tablespoons of honey, mix all ingredients well. Roll on board to one-fourth inch in thickness and cut with form. Brush with white of egg or honey diluted with water. On each cake put an almond or walnut. Bake in moderate oven from fifteen to twenty minutes.

LEBKUCHEN

Four eggs, one pound of brown sugar; beat well. Add one-eighth pound of citron shredded, one-eighth pound of shelled walnuts (broken), one and one-half cups of flour, one teaspoon of baking-powder, two teaspoons of cinnamon, one-fourth teaspoon of allspice. Spread the dough in long pans with well-floured hands, have about one and one-half inches thick. Bake in very moderate oven. When baked, cut in squares and spread with icing. Set in a cool stove or the sun to dry.

It is best to let these cakes and all honey cakes stand a week before using.

OLD-FASHIONED LEBKUCHEN

Heat one cup of molasses, mix it with two cups of brown sugar and three eggs, reserving one white for the icing; add one level teaspoon of baking-soda that has been dissolved in a little milk, then put in alternately a little flour and a cup of milk; now add one tablespoon of mixed spices, half cup of brandy, one small cup each of chopped nuts and citron, and lastly, flour enough to make a stiff batter. Place in shallow pans and bake slowly. When done, cover with icing and cut in squares or strips.

Icing for Lebkuchen.—One cup of powdered sugar added to the beaten white of one egg; flavor with one teaspoon of brandy or lemon juice.

DESSERTS

BOILED CUSTARD

Take two cups of milk, two eggs or the yolks of three eggs, two tablespoons of sugar and one-half teaspoon of vanilla. Put the milk on to heat in a double boiler. Beat the eggs thoroughly with the sugar; into them pour the hot milk, stirring to prevent lumps. Return all to the double boiler and cook until the custard coats the spoon, but no longer. If the mixture should curdle, set the boiler in a pan of cold water and beat with a wire egg-beater until smooth. When the steam passes off add the vanilla, or other flavoring.

In the winter, when eggs are expensive, the custard may be made with one egg and one heaping teaspoon of cornstarch dissolved in a little cold milk.

If desired, the whites of the eggs may be beaten separately and added to the custard after it is cold or beaten with sugar into a meringue.

CARAMEL CUSTARD

Melt one-half cup of sugar until it is light brown in color, add four cups of scalded milk. Beat the eggs, add the milk and sugar, one-quarter teaspoon of salt, one teaspoon of vanilla and bake in cups as directed for cup custard. Serve with caramel sauce.

CUP CUSTARD FOR SIX

Stir until quite light four eggs, yolks and whites, and four tablespoons of sugar; have ready four cups of scalded milk; mix, add pinch of salt and one teaspoon of good vanilla; pour into cups and place cups into pan of boiling water. Put into oven and bake exactly twenty-five minutes.

CHOCOLATE CUSTARD

Beat yolks of three eggs, three tablespoons of sugar till light, dissolve one heaping tablespoon of grated unsweetened chocolate, one tablespoon of sugar and one of hot water. When dissolved, add slowly one pint of milk heated to boiling, pour this hot mixture over the beaten eggs and sugar, cook in double boiler, stirring constantly till it thickens; when cool, flavor with vanilla, and place on ice. When ready to serve, half-fill small punch glasses with the custard, heap over them sweetened whipped cream, flavored; putting on top of each glass, and serve cold.

CHOCOLATE CORNSTARCH PUDDING

Take one quart of milk, one and one-half cups of sugar, seven heaping tablespoons of cocoa, six level tablespoons of cornstarch, one tablespoon of vanilla; place milk and sugar up to boil, when boiling, add cocoa, dissolved to a smooth paste; then add cornstarch dissolved in cold water, let come to a boil, remove from fire and add the vanilla; then place in mold and allow to get cold. Serve with whipped cream.

BLANC MANGE

Heat one quart of milk to boiling point. Dissolve four large tablespoons of cornstarch in a quarter cup of cold milk. Beat two whole eggs with one-half cup of sugar until light, and add a tiny pinch of salt. When the milk begins to boil, add a piece of butter, size of a hickory nut, then pour it over the well-beaten eggs and sugar, mix well, and put back on the stove. Stir until it begins to boil, then stir in the dissolved cornstarch until the custard is very thick. Remove from the fire, flavor with vanilla or lemon, pour into a mold, and set on ice till very cold and firm. Serve with cream.

FLOATING ISLAND

Beat light the yolks of three eggs with one-quarter cup of sugar. Scald a pint of milk, beat up the whites of three eggs very stiff and put them into the boiling milk, a spoonful at a time. Take out the boiled whites and lay them on a platter; now pour the hot milk gradually on the beaten yolks, when thoroughly mixed, return to the fire to boil. When it begins to thicken remove. When cool, flavor with vanilla or bitter almond. Pour into a deep glass dish; put the whites on top, and garnish with jelly or candied fruit. Eat cold.

RED RASPBERRY OR CURRANT FLOAT

Take a half-pint glass of red raspberry or currant juice and mix it with a quarter cup of sugar. Beat the whites of four eggs to a stiff froth and add gradually a quarter cup of powdered sugar. Press the raspberries through a strainer to avoid seeds and by degrees beat the juice with the sugar and eggs until so stiff that it stands in peaks. Chill it thoroughly and serve in a glass dish half filled with cold whipped cream. Heap on the mixture by the spoonful, like floating island. If currant juice is used it will require a pint of sugar.

ROTHE GRITZE

Take one cup of currant juice, sufficiently sweetened, and a pinch of salt. Let this boil and add to it enough cornstarch to render it moderately thick and then boil again for ten minutes. It should be eaten cold with cream. (About one-quarter cup of cornstarch dissolved in cold water will be sufficient to thicken.)

APPLE SNOW

Peel and grate one large sour apple, sprinkling over it three-fourths cup of powdered sugar as it is grated to keep it from turning dark. Add the unbeaten whites of two eggs; beat constantly for half an hour; arrange mound fashion on a glass dish with cold boiled custard around it.

BOHEMIAN CREAM

Stir together and whip one pint of double cream and one pint of grape juice or grape jelly melted, this must be whipped to a froth. Drain if needed. Put in cups and set on ice for several hours. Serve with lady lingers.

PRUNE WHIP

Soak one-half pound of prunes in cold water overnight. In the morning let them simmer in this water until they are very soft. Remove stones and rub through strainer. Add one-half cup of sugar and cook five minutes or until the consistency of marmalade. When the fruit mixture is cold, add the well-beaten whites of three eggs and one-half teaspoon of lemon juice; add this gradually, then heap lightly in buttered dish and bake twenty minutes in a slow oven. Serve cold with thin custard or cream.

RICE CUSTARD

Beat four eggs light with one cup of sugar. Add one cup of cooked rice, two cups of sweet milk, juice and rind of one lemon, one-half teaspoon of cinnamon. Pour in pudding-pan and place in a pan filled with hot water; bake until firm in moderate oven. Serve with lemon sauce.

PRUNE CUSTARD

Heat a little more than a pint of sweet milk to the boiling point, then stir in gradually a little cold milk in which you have rubbed smooth a heaping tablespoon of butter and a little nutmeg. Let this just come to a boil, then pour into a buttered pudding-dish, first adding one cup of stewed prune with the stones taken out. Bake for fifteen to twenty minutes, according to the state of oven. A little cream improves it when it is served in the saucers.

TAPIOCA CUSTARD

Soak four tablespoons of tapioca overnight in one quart of sweet milk. In the morning beat the yolks of three eggs with one cup of sugar. Put the milk and tapioca on in a double boiler, adding a pinch of salt; when this comes to boiling point stir in the eggs and sugar. Beat the whites to a stiff froth and stir quickly and delicately into the hot mixture. Flavor with vanilla. Eat cold.

WHIPPED CREAM

To one pint of rich thick cream add one-quarter of a pound of powdered sugar and one-half teaspoon of vanilla.

Put in a large platter in a cool place and whip with a wire egg-whip until perfectly smooth and velvety. Set on ice until wanted. In the summer set the cream on ice before whipping. A good plan is to set the bowl in another one filled with ice while whipping.

DESSERT WITH WHIPPED CREAM

Line the edges of a mold or a large glass dish with lady fingers and fill up with whipped cream. Ornament with macaroons and candied fruit. Serve cold.

AMBROSIA

Cut up into small pieces different kinds of fruit; then chop up nuts and marshmallows (not too fine). Mix these and sugar, not allowing it to draw too much juice. Flavor with sherry, if you like. Serve individually, putting whipped cream on the top with a cherry.

MACAROON ISLAND

Fill a glass bowl with alternate layers of macaroons and lady fingers, sprinkle a layer of finely-chopped nuts over the cake, then a layer of crystallized cherries.

Boil one cup of wine, one cup of sugar and one-half cup of water together until syrupy and thick, pour it over the contents of the bowl, let this cool, then place a thick layer of thickly-whipped sweetened and flavored cream over all. Serve very cold.

PISTACHIO CREAM

Take out the kernels of half a pound of pistachio nuts and pound them in a mortar with one tablespoon of brandy. Put them in a double boiler with a pint of rich cream and add gradually the yolks of three eggs, well beaten. Stir over the fire until it thickens and then pour carefully into a bowl, stirring as you do so and being careful not to crack the bowl. (Put a silver spoon into the bowl before pouring in the cream, as this will prevent it cracking). When cold, stick pieces of the nuts over the cream and serve.

TIPSY PUDDING

Cut stale sponge cake into thin slices, spread with jelly or preserves, put two pieces together like sandwiches and lay each slice or sandwich on the plate on which it is to be served. Wet each piece with wine, pour or spread a tablespoon of rich custard over each piece of pudding, and then frost each piece with a frosting and put in a moderate oven for a few minutes. Eat cold.

APPLE AND LADY-FINGER PUDDING

Core and peel apples, take top off, chop the top with almonds, citron and raisins; butter your pan, fill apples, sugar them and pour over a little wine, bake until tender; when cool add four yolks of eggs beaten with one cup of sugar, then last, add beaten whites and eight lady fingers rolled, and juice of one whole lemon; pour over apples, bake. Eat cold.

FIG DESSERT

Soak two cups white figs overnight. In the morning boil slowly until tender, add two cups of sugar and boil until a thick syrup is formed. Line a dish with sponge cake or lady fingers; pour the figs in the centre and cover with whipped cream that has been sweetened and flavored. Decorate with candied cherries or angelica.

STRAWBERRIES À LA "BRIDGE"

Into a champagne-glass put large strawberries, halved and sugared, and an equal amount of marshmallows halved. Place on top a mass of whipped cream, already sweetened and flavored then a single strawberry, sprinkle with shelled pecans.

QUEEN OF TRIFLES

Make a rich custard of four eggs, one cup of granulated sugar and one quart of milk to which has been added one teaspoon of cornstarch. Let this cook in double boiler, stirring constantly, until the custard is very thick. Cool.

Soak one-half pound of macaroons in sherry wine, blanch and chop one-quarter pound of almonds, cut fine one-quarter pound of dried figs; one-quarter pound of crystallized cherries and one-half pound of lady fingers are required as well.

Line a deep glass bowl with the lady fingers cut in half, add macaroons, fruit and almonds in layers until all are used. Then pour the boiled custard over all. Set on ice and when cold, fill the bowl with whipped cream that has been sweetened and flavored with vanilla. Decorate with a few cherries.

ICE-BOX CAKE

One-half cup of butter creamed with one-half cup of confectioner's sugar, three whole eggs added, one at a time, beat these all for twenty minutes, add one-half pound of chopped nuts, one tablespoon mocha essence or one square of bitter chocolate melted, or one teaspoon of vanilla.

Grease a spring form, put two dozen lady fingers around the edge, at the bottom put one dozen macaroons, then add the filling and let this all stand for twenty-four hours in ice-box. When ready to serve, pour one-half pint of cream, whipped, over all and serve.

AUFLAUF

Boil one cup of milk and when boiling stir in quickly one-half cup of sifted flour and work smooth until all lumps are out and it is the consistency of soft mashed potatoes. Stir all the while over fire. When smooth remove from stove and while yet warm break in, one by one, yolks of three eggs, a pinch of salt, then the beaten whites of three eggs. Bake in well-buttered hot square pans, in very hot oven, from fifteen to twenty minutes. Serve as soon as done with jelly or preserves. If batter is not thick enough a little more flour must be added to the milk.

LEMON PUFFS

Beat the yolks of four eggs until very light, add the stiffly-beaten whites and then stir in two cups of milk, add a pinch of salt, three tablespoons of fresh butter melted, and five level tablespoons of flour that have been wet with a little of the milk from the pint, stir well together and divide equally between cups. Butter the cups before pouring in the mixture. Bake in hot oven until brown (generally twenty minutes). Turn out carefully in the dish in which they are to be served, and pour over them the following:

LEMON SAUCE

Put on to boil one and one-half cups of water with juice of two lemons, sweeten to taste, add a few small pieces of cinnamon bark; when boiling stir in three teaspoons of cornstarch that have been dissolved in a little cold water. Boil a few minutes, then pour over the well-beaten yolks of two eggs, stirring all the time. Stir in stiffly-beaten whites of eggs, and pour over and around puffs when cold. Serve cold.

LEAF PUFFS

Cream one cup of butter until soft, add two cups of sifted flour, mix well, and add just enough sweet cream to make a nice dough, not too soft. Roll thin, cut in long strips or squares, bake in long pans in a moderately hot oven. When light brown, draw to the door of the oven, sprinkle with powdered sugar and let stand a few minutes longer in the oven.

SAGO PUDDING WITH STRAWBERRY JUICE

Prepare one cup berry juice and sweeten to taste. Have ready a scant half teacup of sago soaked one hour in water enough to cover. Boil the sago in the fruit juice until thick like jelly. Beat up the whites of two eggs and add to the sago while hot and remove immediately from the stove. Mold and serve with cream or berry juice.

This mold can be made with any kind of fruit juice preferred

APPLE TAPIOCA PUDDING

Soak three-quarter cup of tapioca and boil it in one quart of water until clear, sweetening to taste. Pare and core six apples and place them in a baking dish. Fill the cores with sugar, pour the tapioca around them and grate a little nutmeg over the top. Cover and bake until the apples are soft Serve with cream.

RHUBARB PUDDING

Grate some stale rye bread and take a bunch of rhubarb; cut fine without peeling, put the cut rhubarb in a pan with a big pinch of baking-soda, and pour boiling water over to cover. While that is steeping, grate the rye bread and butter pudding-form well, and put crumbs all over the pan about one-quarter inch deep, then add one-half the rhubarb that has been well drained of the water; season with brown sugar, cinnamon, nuts and any other seasoning you like; then some more crumbs, and other one-half of rhubarb, and season as before the top crumbs, put flakes of butter all over top; bake until done.

SCALLOPED PEACHES

Pare a number of peaches and put them whole into a baking-tin, together with layers of bread crumbs and sugar and add a few cloves. Bake until the top is brown. Serve with hot butter sauce or cream.

STEAMED PUDDINGS

The tin molds are best for this purpose, either melon, round, or brick. If the mold is buttered first, then sprinkled with granulated sugar, a nice crust will form. Have a large, deep pan filled with boiling water. Place mold in, let water come up to rim, put a heavy weight on top of mold to keep down, and boil steadily. The pan must be constantly replenished with boiling water, if the pudding is to be done in time. Always place paper in top of mold to prevent water from penetrating. When puddings are boiled in bags, a plate must be placed in bottom of pan to prevent burning. Only certain puddings can be boiled in bags. Always grease inside of bag, so puddings will slip out easily. A bag made of two thicknesses of cheese-cloth, stitched together, will do. Always leave room in mold or bag for pudding to rise, using a smaller or larger mold according to quantity of pudding. If not boiled steadily, and emptied as soon as done, puddings will fall and stick.

ALMOND PUDDING

Beat the yolks of four eggs very light with one-half cup of sugar; then add one-half cup of grated walnuts or almonds, one-half cup of grated white bread crumbs, then the stiffly-beaten whites of four eggs. Put in pudding form and steam from one and one-half to two hours. Serve with wine or fruit sauce.

RYE BREAD PUDDING

Dry one-half cup of rye bread crumbs in oven. Beat the yolks of four eggs very light with one-half cup of sugar, then add a pinch of cloves and allspice, one-half teaspoon of cinnamon, grated rind of one-half lemon and one-quarter pound of chopped almonds. Moisten crumbs with three tablespoons of whiskey or brandy, add to eggs, then add stiffly-beaten whites of four eggs. Put in mold and boil three hours. Serve with a brandy or whiskey sauce.

NAPKIN PUDDING

Soak one-half loaf of stale white bread in water until moist, squeeze perfectly dry. Put in skillet two tablespoons of clear fat or butter, and when hot add bread, and stir until smooth and dry. Beat five eggs light with one cup of sugar, stir bread in, mix well, and flavor with rind (grated) and juice of one lemon. Grease a bag or very large napkin, place pudding in this, tie, leaving plenty room to rise, place in boiling water and boil two hours. Make a jelly sauce, not as thin as usual, and pour over just before serving. If desired one-half cup of currants can be added to pudding.

STEAMED BERRY PUDDING

Take one tablespoon of butter (or other shortening), one-quarter cup of sugar, yolk of one egg, one-half cup of milk, one cup of flour, one teaspoon of baking-powder, one-quarter teaspoon of salt, one-half cup of berries or pitted cherries rolled in flour. Put in a well-greased melon mold and cook in boiling water steadily for two hours. Serve with hard sauce.

CARROT PUDDING

Take one cup of sugar, one-third cup of butter, one cup of grated carrots, one cup of grated potatoes, one cup of raisins, one cup of currants, two cups of bread crumbs, one-half teaspoon of baking-soda stirred in the potatoes, one teaspoon each of cloves, cinnamon, and allspice. Mix all these and add a little syrup and four tablespoons of whiskey. Steam four hours. Serve with hard sauce.

CHERRY PUDDING

Grate one-half pound of stale rye bread and wet this with a wineglass of red wine. Pound two tablespoons of almonds, stir the yolks of four eggs with half a cup of powdered sugar, flavor with cinnamon, and add the grated bread and almonds. Stone one-half pound each of sweet and sour cherries. Mix all thoroughly with the beaten whites added last. Do not take the juice of the cherries. Butter the pudding mold well before you put in the mixture. To be eaten cold.

DATE PUDDING

Melt three tablespoons of butter, add one-half cup of molasses, one-half cup of milk, one and two-third cups of flour sifted with one-half teaspoon of baking-soda, one-quarter teaspoon of salt, one-quarter teaspoon each of cloves, cinnamon, and nutmeg. Add to the above one-half pound of dates, stoned and cut. Turn into a well-buttered mold. Butter the cover also and steam two and one-half hours. Keep at a steady boil. Serve with any kind of sauce.

PRINCE ALBERT PUDDING

Rub to a cream half a pound of sweet butter and half a pound of sifted powdered sugar; add the yolks of six eggs, one at a time, and the grated peel of one lemon. Stone half a pound of raisins, and add also a little citron, cut very fine. Now add gradually half a pound of the finest flour, sifted three or four times, and the stiffly-beaten whites of the eggs. Pour this mixture into a well-buttered mold, into which you have strewn some blanched and pounded almonds. Boil fully three hours. Serve with sweet brandy or fruit sauce.

PEACH PUDDING

In a large mixing bowl whip to a cream two eggs, three tablespoons of sugar, and two tablespoons of butter. To this, after it is well beaten, add a saltspoon of salt and half a grated nutmeg. Stir these ingredients well into the mixture; then stir in a cup of milk. Last add, a little at a time—stirring it well in to make a smooth batter—a cup and a half of flour and three-quarters of a cup of Indian meal, which have been sifted together with three teaspoons of baking-powder in another bowl.

Butter well the inside of a two-quart pudding mold; put a layer of the pudding batter an inch deep in the mold; cover this with a layer of fine ripe peaches that have been peeled and cut in quarters or eighths—this depends upon the size of the peaches. Sprinkle the layer of peaches with a light layer of sugar; then pour in a layer of batter; then a layer of peaches. Repeat this process till all the material is in, leaving a layer of batter on top. Steam for two hours.

NOODLE PUDDING

Make noodles with two eggs. Boil in boiling salt water for ten minutes, drains and set aside.

Beat the yolks of four eggs with one cup of powdered sugar until light, add a quarter of a cup of pounded almonds, a pinch of salt, the drained noodles, and the whites of the eggs beaten to a stiff froth. Mix well, pour into a greased pudding mold, and boil one and one-half hours.

PRUNE PUDDING

Take the yolks of four eggs, a cup of granulated sugar, and stir to a cream. Chop fine thirty prunes (prunes being boiled without sugar), and add two tablespoons of sweet chocolate, two tablespoons of grated almonds, and the whites, which have been beaten to a snow. Boil two and one-half hours in a pudding form and serve with whipped cream.

PLUM PUDDING (FOR THANKSGIVING DAY)

Soak a small loaf of bread; press out every drop of water, work into this one cup of suet shaved very fine, the yolks of six eggs, one cup of currants, one cup of raisins seeded, one-half cup of citron shredded fine, three-quarters cup of syrup, one wineglass of brandy, one cup of sifted flour and the stiffly-beaten whites of eggs last. Boil four hours in greased melon mold.

PLUM PUDDING, No. 2

Chop a half box of raisins and currants, one-quarter pound of citron, one-quarter pound of suet (chopped very fine), two eggs, one and one-half cups of sugar, a wineglass of brandy, two cups of cider, one teaspoon of cinnamon and ground cloves. When all these are well mixed add enough flour (with a teaspoon of baking-powder in it) to thicken well. Cook in a greased mold and allow to steam for three hours.

HONEY PUDDING

Mix one-half cup of honey with six ounces of bread crumbs and add one-half cup of milk, one-half teaspoon of ginger, grated rind of half a lemon and yolks of two eggs. Beat the mixture thoroughly and then add two tablespoons of butter and the whites of the eggs well beaten. Steam for about two hours in a pudding mold which is not more than three-quarters full.

PUDDING SAUCES

BRANDY SAUCE

Take one cup of water, a quarter glass of brandy, one cup of sugar, juice of half a lemon. Boil all in double boiler. Beat the yolks of two eggs light, and add the boiling sauce gradually to them, stirring constantly until thick.

CARAMEL SAUCE

Put one cup cut loaf sugar in a saucepan on the stove without adding a drop of water. Let it melt slowly and get a nice brown without burning.

Beat the yolks of three eggs until light, stir in two cups of sweet milk, and when the sugar is melted, stir all into the saucepan and continue stirring until the sugar is dissolved and the sauce is somewhat thickened; then remove from the fire, add one teaspoon of vanilla essence, put in a bowl and put the stiffly-beaten whites of eggs on top. Serve with puddings, cakes or fritters.

CHOCOLATE SAUCE, No. 1

Dissolve one-half pound chocolate in one cup of water and sugar to taste, boil somewhat thick and flavor with vanilla.

CHOCOLATE SAUCE, No. 2

Scald two cups of milk, add two tablespoons of cornstarch diluted with one-half cup of cold milk, and cook ten minutes over boiling water. Melt three squares of chocolate over hot water, add three tablespoons of sugar and three tablespoons of hot water; stir until smooth, then add to cooked mixture. Beat the whites of three eggs until stiff, add three-fourths of a cup of powdered sugar; add the yolks and stir into cooked mixture; cool and add vanilla.

FOAM SAUCE

Cream one-quarter cup of butter with one cup of powdered sugar, until very light. Add separately the unbeaten whites of two eggs, stirring briskly and beat again. Add one teaspoon of vanilla and one-half cup of hot water. Pour in sauceboat, and place boat in a pan of boiling water on stove, until it becomes frothy then serve immediately.

FRUIT SAUCES

Wash the fruit well, then put on the stove in a saucepan without adding any more water. Cover with a lid, and let the fruit get thoroughly heated all through until it comes to a boil, but do not boil it. Stir occasionally.

When well heated, mash the fruit well with a wooden potato masher, then strain through a fine sieve, being careful to get every drop of substance from the fruit.

Sweeten the juice with sugar to taste, add a few drops of wine or lemon juice, put back on the stove, and cook until it thickens, stirring occasionally. Serve with cake, fritters or puddings.

Blackberries, strawberries or raspberries, make a nice sauce.

HARD SAUCE

Take one cup of sugar, one-half cup of sweet butter and stir to a cream. Flavor with grated lemon peel or essence of lemon. Make into any shape desired and serve.

JELLY SAUCE

Take thin jelly, add one cup boiling water and brandy or wine (one-half cup), add a little more sugar and thicken with one teaspoon cornstarch dissolved in a little cold water. The beaten white of egg may be added.

KIRSCH SAUCE

Put one cup of sugar and two cups of water on to boil. Mix two tablespoons of cornstarch in one-quarter cup of cold water, and when the water in the saucepan is boiling, add cornstarch and stir for two minutes. Remove from stove and add one cup of Kirsch wine and stir again. Strain and serve with pudding.

LEMON SAUCE, No. 1

Boil one cup of sugar with one-half cup of water, rind of one lemon, juice of two, and one-half teaspoon of butter. When boiling stir in a scant teaspoon of cornstarch dissolved in a little cold water. Serve hot. Serve with puddings or fritters.

LEMON SAUCE, No. 2

Boil the strained juice of two lemons and the grated peel of one with a cup of sugar and one glass of white wine or water. When boiled to a syrup add the yolks of three eggs well beaten, also half of the whites beaten to a froth. Use the other half of the stiffly-beaten whites, sweetened with powdered sugar, to decorate the sauce. Serve immediately.

PRUNE SAUCE

Take about one pound of Turkish prunes, wash them in hot water, and put on to boil in cold water. Boil until they are very soft. Remove the pits or kernels, and strain over them the water they were boiled in, sweeten to taste. Flavor with ground cinnamon, then mash them until a soft mush. If too thick, add the juice of an orange.

WINE SAUCE, No. 1

Take one-half cup of white wine and one and one-half cups of water, put on to boil in double boiler and in the meantime beat up the yolks of two eggs very light, with two teaspoons of white sugar, some grated nutmeg or three small pieces of cinnamon bark, or the grated rind of half a lemon, and add a teaspoon of flour to this gradually. When perfectly smooth add the boiling wine, pouring very little at a time and stirring constantly. Return to boiler and stir until the spoon is coated.

WINE SAUCE, No. 2

Melt one tablespoon of butter in a saucepan, stir in one tablespoon of flour, then add one-half cup of cold water, stirring constantly until smooth.

Then add one cup of white wine, one ounce of chopped citron. Remove from fire, let cool, flavor with one teaspoon each of pistache and vanilla. If desired, one teaspoon of red Curaçao or Maraschino liquor can be added for flavoring.

VANILLA OR CREAM SAUCE

Mix one teaspoon cornstarch and one tablespoon of sugar thoroughly; on them slowly pour one cup of scalding milk, stirring all the time. Cook and stir in a double boiler for ten minutes; then set aside to cool. When ready to use stir in one teaspoon of vanilla and the white of one egg, stiffly beaten. Serve in place of whipped cream.

FROZEN DESSERTS

In making frozen desserts attention to detail is the essential thing to perfect success.

PREPARING SALT

The smaller the ice is broken the better, while the salt should never be too fine. A salt prepared especially for the purpose is known as "ice cream salt." This salt and the finely broken ice are put in alternate layers about the cream can. Begin with a layer of ice, making this about three inches deep. Then put in a layer of salt about an inch in depth, and continue in this way up to the top of the cream can. The ice can be put in a gunny sack and then broken up with a heavy hammer or hatchet.

FREEZING CREAMS AND WATER ICES

Fill the cream can three-fourths full. Cover; place in wooden bucket; adjust the top and pack, as directed above. Turn crank slowly and steadily. After freezing drain off water, remove dasher; with a spoon pack hard. Put cork in top of lid. Repack freezer. Cover top with heavy pieces of carpet and paper. When time comes to serve, wipe top of can carefully before opening. In very hot weather renew the salt and ice three times, and keep the blanket cold and wet with the brine from the freezer.

VANILLA ICE CREAM, No. 1

Take one pint of milk, two cups of sugar, one large tablespoon of flour rubbed smooth in cold milk, two eggs beaten light, one teaspoon of vanilla extract, and one quart of sweet cream, well beaten. Heat the milk in a double boiler, and when it is at boiling point add the flour, eggs and one cup of sugar. Cook about twenty minutes, stirring very often. Let the mixture get cold, then add the remaining sugar and the vanilla and cream, and freeze. A more novel flavoring is made with a mixture of vanilla, lemon and almond extracts. The quantities given in this recipe make about two quarts of ice cream.

VANILLA ICE CREAM, No. 2

Beat three whole eggs very light with one cup of granulated sugar until all grain is dissolved and mass is a light yellowish color. Whip one pint of cream until stiff, add to eggs and sugar, then add one cup of sweet milk, flavor with vanilla to taste, and put in freezer and turn until hard. This is a basis for almost any kind of cream.

CHOCOLATE ICE CREAM, No. 1

Make same as Vanilla Ice Cream, No. 2, only omitting the milk. Dissolve on stove one-half pound of sweet chocolate, in one cup of sweet milk, rub smooth and thick, let get cold, and add to the eggs, just before putting in cream. Flavor with vanilla.

CHOCOLATE ICE CREAM, No. 2

Take one quart of cream, one pint of new milk, two eggs, one teacup of grated chocolate (double vanilla), two cups of pulverized sugar, one teaspoon of cornstarch and one of extract of vanilla. Beat the yolks of the eggs, sugar and let them come to a boil. Then take them quickly from the fire, dissolve the chocolate in a little milk over the fire, stir it all the time. When smooth mix with the milk and eggs, add the cream and vanilla. Freeze when cold.

COFFEE ICE CREAM

Make same as Vanilla Ice Cream No. 2. Flavor with one and one-half tablespoons of mocha extract, add one cup of grated walnuts. Freeze.

FROZEN CUSTARD

One quart of milk, yolk of five eggs, sweeten to taste, and flavor with vanilla to taste. Boil the milk first, and after the yolks of eggs are beaten stir into the milk. When cold add the beaten whites and vanilla; put in freezer and turn. Canned strawberries are very nice in this.

APRICOT, PEACH, STRAWBERRY, BANANA OR PINEAPPLE CREAM

Make same as Vanilla Ice Cream No. 2, omitting the milk. If canned fruit is to be used, drain off the juice, and add it to the eggs and cream. Mash the fruit through a sieve, add it to rest of mixture, and freeze the whole. If fresh fruits are used, one pint is required. Mash fine, strain and sweeten before adding to the cream. For peach and strawberry a few drops of pink coloring may be added. Bananas must be mashed smooth, but not sweetened. Chop all fruits very fine For pineapple, the sliced is preferred to the grated. Either canned or fresh can be used.

TUTTI-FRUTTI ICE CREAM

Take three pints of cream, one pound of pulverized sugar and the yolks of nine eggs. Prepare just like the other creams. When half frozen add one-half pound of crystallized fruit, peaches, apricots, cherries, citron, etc., chopped very fine. Put in also a wineglass of pale sherry and the juice of an orange or lemon. Finish freezing.

FROZEN PUDDINGS

For frozen puddings ice must be crushed and mixed with rock-salt, the same way as for freezing cream. Pudding-mold must have a tight cover; have a receptacle sufficiently large to line bottom and sides with a thick layer of mixed salt and ice. Put the mold in the centre, fill with the pudding, cover tightly, then put ice on top and all around. Put a sheet of plain tissue paper in top of mold to prevent salt from penetrating. Cover whole with a cloth and let freeze from three to four hours.

BISCUIT TORTONI, No. 1

Take one-half cup of granulated sugar, one-fourth pound of stale macaroons grated, one-half pint of heavy cream (whipped), three eggs, vanilla or sherry wine. Stir yolks of eggs until thick and add sugar and stir again; add whipped cream, and whipped whites of eggs, and grated macaroons; flavor to taste. Put this all into freezer and pack outside with ice and salt alternately. Do not turn. Let stand five or six hours, adding ice from time to time. When serving put grated macaroons on top.

BISCUIT TORTONI, No. 2

Take yolks of two eggs, one pint of cream, eight macaroons, vanilla and flavor, one-half cup of sugar, one-half cup of milk. Beat yolks of eggs and the sugar very light. Put on milk to a boil, and when it comes to a boil stir into the beaten eggs and sugar and set away to cool. Beat cream and add macaroons, leaving just enough to put in the bottom of your form. When your custard is cool, add cream, put all in forms, pack and freeze two hours or longer.

MOCHA MOUSSE

Cream yolks of three eggs with one-half cup of granulated sugar. Add one-half pint of cream, whipped; one-half cup of grated macaroons, two tablespoons of mocha essence, one teaspoon of vanilla, lastly beaten whites. Put in a mold and pack in salt and ice for three hours.

MAPLE MOUSSE

Whip one pint of cream until quite thick. Break two eggs into another bowl, beat until light and add gradually, one-half cup of maple syrup. When the two are well mixed, whip them gradually into the cream. Pour the whole into a freezer can, without the dasher; cover; pack in ice and salt, and let stand for three hours.

MAPLE BISQUE

Boil one cup of maple syrup until quite thick; beat yolks of three eggs; add to syrup while hot, stirring constantly until well mixed. Let cool. Beat whites of eggs to a froth. Whip one pint of cream, mix all together; add one-half cup of chopped nuts. Have a pudding-mold buttered; see that the edges fit close. Pack in rock salt and ice four hours.

FROZEN CREAM CHEESE WITH PRESERVED FIGS

Take three Neufchatel cheeses. Mash the cheese to a smooth paste and add one-half cup of thick cream, one-half teaspoon of salt, one rounding teaspoon of sugar. Place in a small square mold, bury in salt and ice and let stand several hours. When ready to serve unmold, cut in squares, place each on a lettuce leaf, decorate the centre of the cheese square with a preserved fig and serve at once.

RUM PUDDING

Beat yolks of two eggs with one-half cup of sugar until light, then add stiffly-beaten whites. Flavor with one tablespoon of rum. Whip one pint of cream very stiff, stir into beaten eggs. Line a melon mold with lady fingers, split in half. Then put a layer of whipped cream over. Chop one-half pound of marron glacé fine and sprinkle some over cream. Put another layer of lady fingers, cream and marrons, and so on until mold is filled. Close tightly, and pack in rock salt and ice, from three to four hours.

CHERRY DIPLOMATE

Line a mold with white cake, thinly sliced, which you have previously dipped in maraschino or some other fine brandy. Then fill in with plain white ice-cream, then a layer of cherry ice, next a layer of candied cherries, next a layer of cherry-ice then a layer of strawberry ice-cream or the plain white vanilla. Finish it up with a layer of cake again and be sure to dip the cake in maraschino. Cover all up tight and pack in ice until wanted.

NESSELRODE PUDDING

Put on one-half pound of shelled and skinned chestnuts in cold water, and let them boil until very tender, then press them through a purée sieve. Beat the yolks of five eggs with one-half pound of sugar until light, then add the mashed chestnuts, then stir in one pint of sweet cream. Put on to boil in a double boiler, add a few grains of salt, and stir until the mixture begins to boil, then remove at once from fire and set aside to cool. In a bowl put one-fourth pound of crystallized cherries, cut in half; one-fourth pound of crystallized pineapple cut up, one ounce of citron cut fine, one-fourth cup of stoned raisins and one-half cup of maraschino cordial. Put the chestnut cream in a freezer, freeze ten minutes, then add one pint cream that has been whipped stiff with two tablespoons of powdered sugar, turn until it begins to get stiff, then add the fruits and turn awhile longer. Pack in a pudding-mold in rock salt and ice two hours.

CANNED FRUIT FROZEN

Without opening, pack a can of pears in ice and salt, as for ice-cream. Let it remain for three or four hours. When taken out, cut the can open around the middle. If frozen very hard, wrap around with a towel dipped in hot water; the contents can then be clipped out in perfect rounds. Cut into slices and serve with a spoonful of whipped cream on each slice. This will serve six or eight persons.

Canned peaches may be used if desired.

PETER PAN DESSERT

Cut a banana in four strips, cross two over two in basket-shape, fill centre square with a tablespoon of ice-cream and sprinkle over all some chopped walnuts, pistachio nuts and marshmallows, cut in strips.

FRUIT SHERBETS

There is no form in which ices are more palatable or healthful than in the form of sherbet. This is made of fruit juice, sugar and water. The simplest sherbet is made by mixing the sugar, water and fruit juice together. A richer and smoother ice is obtained by boiling the sugar and water together, then adding the fruit juice, and when the mixture is cool, freezing it. It takes nearly twice as long to freeze the preparation made in this way as when made with the uncooked mixture.

Sherbets are usually served at the end of a dinner, but they are sometimes served before the roast.

APRICOT ICE

Pare and grate one dozen apricots, and blanch a few of the kernels. Then pound them and add to the grated fruit. Pour a pint of water over them, adding the juice of a lemon also. Let them stand for an hour and strain, adding one-half pound of sugar just before freezing.

LEMON ICE

Take six large, juicy lemons and grate peel of three lemons; two oranges, juice of both, and peel of one; squeeze out every drop of juice and steep the grated peel of lemon and orange in juice for an hour. Strain and mix in one pint of sugar. Stir until dissolved and freeze.

LEMON GINGER SHERBET

Shave very thin bits of the yellow peel from two lemons, being careful not to get any of the white. Cut eight lemons (using the first two) into halves, extract seeds and press out the juice. Cut one-fourth pound of ginger in strips. Boil until clear, four cups of sugar, two quarts of boiling water, ginger and shaved lemon peel. Add lemon juice and strain through a cheese-cloth. Freeze until thick and add the stiff-beaten whites of two eggs. Mix well; finish freezing, and pack.

ORANGE ICE

Make a syrup of two cups of sugar and four cups of water. Boil fifteen minutes and add two cups of orange juice, one-half cup of lemon juice and the grated rind of one orange and one lemon. Freeze and serve in glasses.

PINEAPPLE ICE

Make a syrup of four cups of water, two cups of sugar and boil fifteen minutes. Add one can grated pineapple and juice of six lemons. Cool and add four cups of ice-water. Freeze until mushy, using half ice and half salt.

PUNCH ICES

To the juice of two lemons take three-quarters of a pound of loaf sugar, two or three tablespoons of rum and one pint of water. Rub the rind of the lemons onto the sugar, then boil the sugar and water together for fifteen minutes, add the lemon juice and rum, mix well, strain, and set aside to cool. Then put the mixture into the freezing can and freeze till set.

RASPBERRY ICE

Make a strong lemonade, add raspberry juice to taste, and some grated pineapple. Put into freezer and turn like ice cream and pack, and let stand five hours.

WATERMELON SHERBET

Take good, pale sherry and boil down to quite a thick syrup, with loaf sugar; and then allow to cool. When cold mix with the chopped meat of a very fine, sweet melon, use only the heart of the soft red part, not any near the white rind. Freeze in a freezer as you would ice, but do not allow it to get too hard. Serve in glasses. You may use claret instead of the sherry. If you do, spice it while boiling with whole spices, such as cloves and cinnamon. Strain before adding to the melon.

CAFÉ À LA GLACÉ

Take five tablespoons of fresh-roasted and ground coffee. Pour four cups of boiling water over it; cover quickly and put on the back of the stove, and add one-half pound of sugar. When cold, press through a sieve, and fill in the can to be frozen. Let it remain in freezer five minutes longer before you begin to turn the freezer. Serve in glasses, and put sweetened whipped cream on the top.

CANDIES AND SWEETS

WHITE FONDANT

Used as a foundation for all cream candies.

Put two and one-half cups of granulated sugar in a saucepan, add three-fourths cup of hot water and one-half saltspoon of tartar. Stir until sugar is dissolved, but no longer. Boil without stirring until, when tried in cold water, it will form a soft ball. Wash down the edges of the pan with the finger first dipped in cold water, as the sugar boils up. Pour slowly on greased pan or marble slab. Cool slightly; beat with a wooden spoon until white and creamy. As soon as large lumps appear, it should be kneaded with the hands until smooth. Place in bowl and cover with waxed paper, let it stand overnight in a cool place. If covered and kept in a cool place this will keep for days. Form into bonbons, color and flavor any desired way; dip in melted chocolate, to which has been added a small piece of wax or paraffine. In fact the bonbons may be used in any desired way.

DIVINITY

Boil two cups of granulated sugar, one-half cup of corn syrup and one-half cup of water until it will thread. Beat into the stiff whites of two eggs; add one cup of nuts. Beat until cool and thick. Pour out, cool, and when set, cut into squares.

FUDGE

Boil together two cups of granulated sugar, one-eighth teaspoon of salt and one cup of milk or cream, until when tried in cold water, it will form a soft ball (about eight minutes). Add one-half a cake of Baker's chocolate, two tablespoons of butter and one teaspoon of vanilla. Beat until smooth and creamy; pour into greased pans; cool and cut in squares.

PINOCHE

Take one cup of (packed) medium brown sugar, one-quarter cup of cream, one-third cup of nut meats, one-quarter pound pecans, weighed in shell, and one-third pound hickory in shell. Cook sugar and cream to soft ball test. Cool until you can bear your hand on bottom of pan. Stir until it begins to thicken, add chopped nuts; and when it is too thick to pour easily, spread quickly on a buttered pan, cut in squares and cool.

FRUIT LOAF

Chop coarsely one-half cup of raisins, one-half cup of nuts, one-half cup figs or dates, add enough honey or corn syrup to make a stiff loaf, about two tablespoons. Place in ice-box for one hour, slice and serve in place of candy, rolling each slice in cornstarch.

GLACÉ FOR CANDIES

Boil one pound of sugar with one-half pint of water until it ropes; then add one-half cup of vinegar and boil until it hardens. Dip in fruit, orange slices, nuts or green grapes with stems on, and put aside on a buttered platter to set.

ORANGE CHIPS

Can be made after the fruit has been used. Halve, scoop out, then scrape inside; lay the peel in salt water overnight. Make syrup of two cups of sugar and one cup of water. When boiled thick, cut orange-peel in small strips and drop them into boiling liquid, letting them remain about ten minutes. Remove strips carefully, spreading them on waxed paper to dry.

Grape-fruit rind may be used as well as that of oranges.

CANDIED CHERRIES, PINEAPPLE AND OTHER FRUITS

Boil, but do not stir, one-half pound of loaf sugar in one breakfast cup of water. Pit some cherries, or prepare any desired fruit, and string them on a thread, then dip them in the syrup; suspend them by the thread. When pineapples are used, slice them crosswise and dry them on a sieve or in the open air; oranges should be separated into sections and dried like pineapple.

STUFFED DATES

Make a cut the entire length of dates and remove stones. Fill cavities with English walnuts, blanched almonds, pecans or with a mixture of chopped nuts, and shape in original form. Roll in granulated sugar or powdered sugar and serve on small plate or bonbon dish.

DATES STUFFED WITH GINGER AND NUTS

Remove the stones from choice dates, and chop together equal measures of preserved ginger and blanched nuts chopped, (hickory, pecan, or almond). Mix with fondant or a paste of confectioner's sugar and ginger syrup. Use only enough fondant or paste to hold the ingredients together. With this mixture fill the open space in the dates, cover securely, and roll in granulated sugar.

DATES STUFFED WITH FONDANT

Fill with fondant, letting it project slightly, and insert in it a pecan or half a walnut. Roll in granulated sugar.

STUFFED FIGS

Cut a slit in the side of dried figs, take out some of the pulp with the tip of a teaspoon. Mix with one-fourth cup of the pulp, one-fourth cup of finely-chopped crystallized ginger, a teaspoon of grated orange or lemon rind and a tablespoon of lemon juice. Fill the figs with the mixture, stuffing them so that they look plump.

STUFFED PRUNES

Take one pound of best prunes, stone and soak in sherry for about an hour (do not cover with the wine). Fill prunes with one large browned almond and one-half marshmallow or with another prune, roll in granulated sugar, and when all are finished, put in oven for two or three minutes.

FROSTED CURRANTS

Pick fine, even, large bunches of red currants (not too ripe) and dip each bunch, one at a time, into a mixture of frothed white of egg, then into a thick, boiled sugar syrup. Drain the bunches by laying on a sieve, and when partly dry dip again into the boiled syrup. Repeat the process a third time; then sprinkle powdered sugar over them and lay on a sheet of paper in a slightly warm oven to dry. Used on extra occasions for ornamenting charlottes, cakes, creams, etc.

BEVERAGES

All drinks contain a large proportion of water which is the beverage nature has provided for man. Water for hot drinks should be freshly boiled, freshly drawn water should be used for cold drinks.

COFFEE

Coffee should be bought in small quantities and kept in air-tight cans, and freshly ground as needed. To have perfect coffee, use an earthen or china pot, and have the water boiling when turned onto the coffee. Like tea, the results will not be right if the water is allowed to fall below the boiling point before it is used. Have the coffee ground to a fine powder in order to get its full flavor as well as strength.

BOILED COFFEE

Allow one tablespoon of coffee to each cup of boiling water. Mix coffee with two tablespoons of cold water. Clean egg shells and put in the pot. Allow this to come to a boil and add boiling water, bring to a boil and boil for one minute; add a tablespoon of cold water to assist the grounds in settling. Stand the pot where it will keep hot, but not boil, for five minutes; then serve at once, as coffee allowed to stand becomes flat and loses its aroma. Most cooks use a clean shell or a little of the white of an egg if they do not use the whole. Others beat the whole egg, with a little water, but use only a part of it, keeping the rest for further use in a covered glass in the ice-chest. Cream is usually served with coffee, but scalded milk renders the coffee more digestible than does cream. Fill the cup one-fourth full of hot scalded milk; pour on the freshly made coffee, adding sugar.

FILTERED COFFEE

Place one cup of finely ground coffee in the strainer of the percolator; place the strainer in the pot and place over the heat. Add gradually six cups of boiling water and allow it to filter. Serve at once.

TURKISH COFFEE

For making this the coffee must be pulverized, and it should be made over an alcohol lamp with a little brass Turkish pot. Measure into your pot as many after-dinner coffee cups of water as you wish cups of coffee. Bring the water to a boil and drop a heaping teaspoon of the powdered coffee to each cup on top of the water and allow it to settle. Add one, two or three coffeespoons of powdered sugar, as desired. Put the pot again over the flame; bring the coffee to a boil three times, and pour into the cups. The grounds of the coffee are of course thick in the liquid, so one lets the coffee stand a moment in the cup before drinking.

FRENCH COFFEE

Have your coffee ground very fine and use a French drip coffee-pot. Instead of pouring through water, pour milk through, brought just to the boiling point. The milk passes through slowly, and care must be taken not to let scum form on the milk.

COFFEE FOR TWENTY PEOPLE

Add and mix one pound of coffee finely ground, with one egg and enough cold water to thoroughly moisten it, cover and let stand several hours. Place in thin bag and drop in seven quarts of boiling water. Boil five minutes, let stand ten minutes. Add cream to coffee and serve.

After-dinner coffee is made double the strength of boiled coffee and is served without cream or milk.

BREAKFAST COCOA

Mix two tablespoons prepared cocoa with two tablespoons of sugar and a few grains of salt, dilute with one-half cup of boiling water to make a smooth paste, then add one-half cup of boiling water and boil five minutes, turn into three cups of scalded milk and beat two minutes, using Dover beater and serve.

RECEPTION COCOA

Stir one cup of boiling water gradually onto two tablespoons of cocoa, two tablespoons of sugar and one teaspoon of cornstarch, a few grains of salt (that have been well mixed) in a saucepan; let boil five minutes, stirring constantly. Heat three cups of milk in a double boiler, add the cocoa mixture and one-half teaspoon of vanilla; beat with egg-beater until foamy and serve hot in chocolate cups, with a tablespoon of whipped cream on top of each cup, or take the cheaper marshmallows, place two in each cup and fill cups two-thirds full of hot cocoa.

HOT CHOCOLATE

Scrape two ounces of unsweetened chocolate very fine, add three tablespoons of sugar, small piece of stick cinnamon and one cup of boiling water; stir over moderate heat until smooth, then add three cups of hot milk. Return to the fire for a minute, do not let it boil, remove, add one teaspoon of vanilla. Beat with an egg-beater and serve.

CHOCOLATE SYRUP

Dissolve two cups of sugar in one cup of water and boil five minutes. Mix one cup of cocoa with one cup of water and add to the boiling syrup. Boil slowly for ten minutes, add salt; cool and bottle for further use. This syrup will keep a long time in the ice-chest in summer and may be used for making delicious drinks.

CHOCOLATE NECTAR

Put into a glass two tablespoons of chocolate syrup, a little cream or milk and chopped ice, and fill up the glass with soda water, apollinaris, or milk. Drop a little whipped cream on top.

ICED CHOCOLATE

Follow recipe for boiled chocolate, but do not beat, add one egg, finely chopped ice and three-fourths cup of milk, put in a bowl and beat thoroughly with a Dover beater or pour into jar with cover and shake thoroughly. Serve in tall glasses.

ICED COFFEE

Take boiled coffee, strain, add sugar to taste and chill. When ready to serve, add one quart of coffee, one-half cup of cream and pour in pitcher. Serve in tall glasses. Have ready a small bowl of whipped cream and, if desired, place a tablespoon on top of each glass.

TEA

Scald the tea-pot. Allow one teaspoon of tea to each person, and one extra. When the water boils, pour off the water with which the pot was scalded, put in the tea, and pour boiling water over it. Let it draw three minutes. Tea should never be allowed to remain on the leaves. If not drunk as soon as it is drawn, it should be poured off into another hot tea-pot, or into a hot jug, which should stand in hot water.

TEA (RUSSIAN STYLE)

Use a small earthenware tea-pot, thoroughly clean. Put in two teaspoons of tea leaves, pour over it boiling water to one-fourth of the pot, and let it stand three minutes. Then fill the pot entirely with boiling water and let it stand five minutes. In serving dilute with warm water to suit taste, or serve cold, but always without milk. A thin slice of lemon or a few drops of lemon juice is allowed for each cup. Preserved strawberries, cherries or raspberries are considered an improvement.

RUSSIAN ICED TEA

Make tea for as many cups as desired, strain and cool. Place in ice-box, chill thoroughly and serve in tall glass with ice and flavor with loaf sugar, one teaspoon of rum or brandy, one slice of lemon or one teaspoon preserved strawberries, raspberries, cherries or pineapple, or loaf sugar may be flavored with lemon or orange and packed and stored in jars to be used later to flavor and sweeten the tea. Wash the rind of lemon or orange and wipe dry, then rub over all sides of the sugar.

HOT WINE (GLUEH)

Mix one quart claret, one pint water, two cups of sugar, one-half teaspoon of whole cloves, one teaspoon of whole cinnamon, lemon rind cut thin and in small pieces. Boil steadily for fifteen minutes and serve hot.

FRUIT DRINKS

The success of lemon-, orange- and pineapple-ades depends upon the way they are made. It is best to make a syrup, using one cup of granulated sugar to one cup of water. Put the sugar in cold water over the fire; stir until the sugar is dissolved; then cook until the syrup spins a fine thread. Take from the fire and add the fruit juices while the syrup is hot. If lemonade is desired, lemon should predominate, but orange or pineapple juice or both should be added to yield the best result. Small pieces of fresh pineapple, fresh strawberries and maraschino cherries added at time of serving will make the drink look pretty and will improve the flavor. Shaved or very finely cracked ice should be used.

PINEAPPLE LEMONADE

Pare and grate a ripe pineapple; add the juice of four lemons and a syrup made by boiling together for a few minutes two cups of sugar and the same quantity of water. Mix and add a quart of water. When quite cold strain and ice. A cherry, in each glass is an agreeable addition, as are a few strawberries or raspberries.

QUICK LEMONADE

Wash two lemons and squeeze the juice; mix thoroughly with four tablespoons of sugar, and when the sugar is dissolved add one quart of water, cracked ice, and a little fresh fruit or slices of lemon if convenient.

If the cracked ice is very finely chopped and put in the glasses just before serving it will make a better-looking lemonade. When wine is used take two-thirds water and one-third wine.

LEMONADE IN LARGE QUANTITIES

Take one dozen lemons, one pound of sugar and one gallon of water to make lemonade for twenty people.

FRUIT PUNCH FOR TWENTY PEOPLE

Take one pineapple, or one can of grated pineapple, one cup of boiling water, two cups of freshly made tea (one heaping tablespoon of Ceylon tea, steep for five minutes); one dozen lemons, three oranges sliced and quartered, one quart bottle apollinaris water, three cups of sugar boiled with one and one-half cups of water six to eight minutes, one quart of water, ice. Grate the pineapple, add the one cup of boiling water, and boil fifteen minutes. Strain through jelly-bag, pressing out all the juice; let cool, and add the lemon and orange juice, the tea and syrup. Add apollinaris water just before serving. Pieces of pineapple, strawberries, mint-leaves or slices of banana are sometimes added as a garnish.

MILK LEMONADE

Dissolve in one quart of boiling water two cups of granulated sugar, add three-fourths of a cup of lemon juice, and lastly, one and a half pints of milk. Drink hot or cold with pounded ice.

EGG LEMONADE

Break two eggs and beat the whites and yolks separately. Mix juice of two lemons, four tablespoons of sugar, four cups of water and ice as for lemonade; add the eggs; pour rapidly back and forth from one pitcher to another and serve before the froth disappears.

MARASCHINO LEMONADE

Take the juice of four lemons, twelve tablespoons of sugar, eight cups of water, one cup of maraschino liquor and a few cherries.

ORANGEADE

Take four large, juicy oranges and six tablespoons of sugar Squeeze the oranges upon the sugar, add a very little water and let them stand for fifteen minutes; strain and add shaved ice and water, and a little lemon juice.

CLABBERED MILK

One of the most healthful drinks in the world is clabbered milk; it is far better in a way for every one than buttermilk for it requires no artificial cult to bring it to perfection. The milk is simply allowed to stand in a warm place in the bottles just as it is bought, and when it reaches the consistency of a rich cream or is more like a jelly the same as is required for cheese, it is ready to drink. Pour it into a glass, seasoning it with a little salt, and drink it in the place of buttermilk.

COLD EGG WINE

To each glass of wine allow one egg, beat up, and add sugar to taste. Add wine gradually and grated nutmeg. Beat whites separately and mix.

SODA CREAM

Take three pounds of granulated sugar and one and one-half ounces of tartaric acid, both dissolved in one quart of hot water. When cold add the well-beaten whites of three eggs, stirring well. Bottle for use. Put two large spoonfuls of this syrup in a glass of ice-water, and stir in it one-fourth of a teaspoon of bicarbonate of soda. Any flavor can be put in this syrup.

MULLED WINE

Put cinnamon and allspice (to taste) in a cup of hot water to steep. Add three eggs well beaten with sugar. Heat to a boil a pint of wine, then add spice and eggs. Stir for three minutes and serve.

STRAWBERRY SHERBET

Crush a quart of ripe strawberries, pour a quart of water over them, and add the juice of two lemons. Let this stand about two hours, then strain over a pound of sugar, stir until the sugar is dissolved, and then set upon ice. You may add one tablespoon of rose-water. Serve with chopped ice.

DELICIOUS AND NOURISHING SUMMER DRINK

Pare thinly the rind of three large lemons, put it into a large jug with one pound of raisins stoned and finely chopped, one pound of sugar, and the juice of the lemons. Add one gallon of boiling water, leave to stand for five days, stirring well every day. Then strain and bottle for use.

SHERRY COBBLER

It is best to mix this in a large bowl and fill in glasses just before serving, and put a little of each kind of fruit in each goblet with pounded ice. To begin with, cut pineapple in slices and quarters, a few oranges and a lemon, sliced thin; one cup of powdered sugar and one tumbler of sherry wine. A few berries, such as black and red raspberries, and blackberries are a nice addition. Cover the fruit with the sugar, laid in layers at the bottom of your bowl with pounded ice; add the wine and twice as much water as wine; stir all up well before serving.

CLARET CUP

Squeeze into a glass pitcher the strained juice of one and one-half lemons, add two tablespoons of powdered sugar, one tablespoon of red curaçao; then pour in three cups of claret, and one cup of apollinaris water. Mix thoroughly, add a few slices of orange or pineapple, or both, and a few maraschino cherries. Cut the rinds from two cucumbers without breaking them, hang them on the inside of the pitcher from the top; drop in a good-sized lump of ice and serve at once in thin glasses. Place a bunch of mint at the top of the pitcher.

CORDIAL

Two quarts of water and two and three-quarter pounds of sugar. Boil thirty minutes. Take off stove and add one quart of alcohol. Color and flavor to taste.

EGG-NOG

Separate the whites and yolks of the eggs. To each yolk add one tablespoon of sugar and beat until very light. Beat whites to a stiff froth. One egg is required for each glass of egg-nog. Add two tablespoons of brandy or rum, then one-half cup of milk or cream to each glass, lastly the whites of the eggs. Pour in glass, put a spoon of whipped cream over and grated nutmeg on top.

UNFERMENTED GRAPE JUICE

Wash and stem ten pounds of Concord grapes, put them in a preserving kettle and crush slightly. Bring to the boiling point and cook gently for one-half hour. Strain through cheese-cloth or jelly bag, pressing out all the juice possible; return to fire and with two pounds of sugar conk for fifteen minutes; strain again, reheat and pour into sterilized bottles thoroughly heated. Put in sterilized corks and dip the necks of the bottles in hot sealing-wax. If you can get the self-sealing bottles, the work of putting up grape juice will be light. Sterilize bottles and corks.

www.ingramcontent.com/pod-product-compliance
Lightning Source LLC
Chambersburg PA
CBHW081626100526
44590CB00021B/3615